GOLD AND SILVER

FROM THIS EARTH

William Russell

The Rourke Corporation, Inc.
Vero Beach, Florida 32964

© 1994 The Rourke Corporation, Inc.

PHOTO CREDITS
© William Russell: title page, p. 7, 18, 21; courtesy Handy &
Harman: p. 4, 10, 15; courtesy Alaska Division of Tourism:
p. 12; courtesy Homestake Mining Company: p. 8,13, 17; courtesy
Florida Divsion of Tourism: cover

Library of Congress Cataloging-in-Publication Data

Russell, William, 1942–
    Gold and silver / by William Russell.
        p. cm. — (From this earth)
    Includes index
    ISBN 0-86593-359-6
    1. Gold—Juvenile literature. 2. Silver—Juvenile literature.
[1. Gold. 2.Silver.]
I. Title II. Series.
TN761.6.R87 1994
553.4' 1—dc20   94–504
                                                         CIP
Printed in the USA   AC

TABLE OF CONTENTS

GOLD

Gold is a glittering, yellowish metal found in nature. It is both beautiful and rare. These qualities make gold very valuable. Gold has been prized by people for thousands of years.

Gold is a soft metal, compared to other metals. It can be hammered into sheets thinner than most paper!

Some of the earliest Europeans who came to North and South America were seeking gold. Spanish gold hunters shipped thousands of pounds of gold from the Americas back to Spain.

Gold can be hammered and drawn into fine threads

GOLD ORE

Gold is usually found mixed with other **minerals**. Minerals are the 3,000 or so kinds of solid things that make up the Earth's crust.

Gold **ore** is any combination of minerals that includes some gold. Gold is usually found in rocks, which are themselves combinations of minerals.

Gold can sometimes be found by itself. Gold hunters find gold flakes, grains and chunks called **nuggets**. Most nuggets fit easily in a hand. One nugget in Australia would have barely fit in a suitcase. It weighed 152 pounds and was worth about $1,000,000.

Gold nuggets are prized for their beauty and value

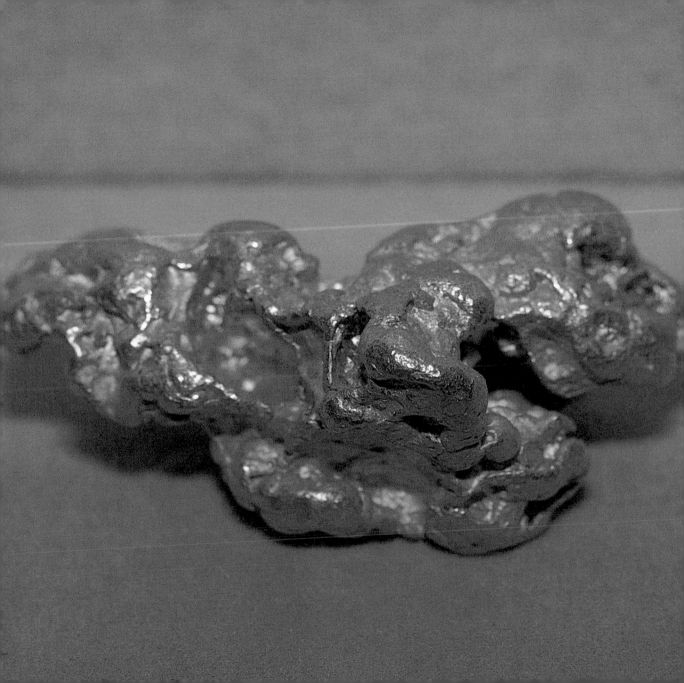

FINDING GOLD

Most gold is removed from ore by heavy machines. The ore is taken from **mines**—holes dug into ground or mountainsides. In some places, gold is collected from gravel and mud.

A few people still **prospect**, or search, for gold on their own. Some of these prospectors **pan** for gold. They sift water and gravel through holes in a pan. Sometimes gold nuggets and flakes are left behind.

More gold is mined in South Africa than anywhere else.

Gold miners with heavy machines work underground mines

USING GOLD

Gold melts when it is heated at high temperatures. Before it hardens, gold can be poured into various shapes, such as bars or candlesticks. People have been shaping gold jewelry and ornaments for at least 5,500 years.

People who work with gold sometimes mix gold with other metals. The mixture is called a gold **alloy**. Gold alloys are harder and stronger than pure gold.

Melted by heat, gold becomes liquid and can be poured

Finding gold in Alaska the old-fashioned way: panning for it

Hot, liquid gold is poured into bars

SILVER

Other than color, silver has many things in common with gold. Silver, too, is a shiny metal. Silver is not quite as soft as gold. But like gold, silver can be easily shaped and hammered thin.

Silver is a very valuable metal. Like gold, it is beautiful and difficult to find. Sometimes gold and silver **veins**, or deposits, are found together.

Like gold, silver is a soft metal that can be shaped easily

SILVER ORE

Silver is usually found in combinations with other metals and minerals. Mixtures of silver and such metals as copper and zinc are common silver ores.

Miners gather silver ore with powerful tools and machines. Pure silver is separated from the ore by several means. Ore may be crushed, melted or treated with certain chemicals.

Miners use machinery to collect ore from rock

FINDING SILVER

Geologists are scientists who study rocks and minerals. They can often guess where a vein of silver will be. They make wise guesses by locating the kinds of rocks and minerals with which silver usually mixes. Miners then dynamite rocks away to see if silver is present.

Mexico produces more silver than any other country. The United States and Canada mine large amounts of silver, too.

Some of the silver mined in the United States is used to produce coins for collectors

USING SILVER

Silver is an important metal because it has many uses. Silver jewelry and tooth fillings are well known, but silver has many "hidden" uses.

Silver is important in the processing of film. Silver wires carry electric current. Hospitals and doctors use special items made of silver. Some batteries are made with certain silver parts.

Metals—gold and silver, for instance—are not alike. Each metal has certain things about it which make it useful to people. Silver has more uses than most metals.

*People have made silver jewelry for
hundreds of years*

GOLD AND SILVER MONEY

Gold and silver were the first metals used as coins. People in Lydia, now the country of Turkey, used coins that were a mixture of gold and silver 2,500 years ago.

The United States government used to **mint**, or make, gold coins called "eagles." The last eagles were minted in 1933. Canada and the United States still mint gold coins for gold collectors. The value of these coins changes each day, so they are not used for money.

American coins in common use as money are made of metals other than silver and gold.

Glossary

alloy (AH loy) — a mixture of two or more metals

geologist (gee AHL uh gist) — scientist who studies rocks, minerals, earthquakes, volcanoes and land forms

mine (MINE) — a hole or tunnel dug into rock or soil for the purpose of removing materials, such as gold, silver or coal

mineral (MIN er uhl) — any of several natural, non-living materials which occur in the Earth

mint (MINT) — to produce money; the factory where money is made

nugget (NUH git) — a lump of precious metal, especially gold

ore (OR) — rock or metal of which a part is a valuable material

pan (PAN) — to use a pan to separate gold from gravel and water

prospect (PRAH spekt) — to search for something, especially a valuable metal or mineral

vein (VANE) — a deposit or layer of a valuable metal or rock

INDEX